Momentum Builders

228 Sure Fire Ways To Get on a Roll. . .and Stay There

by
John Mason

Tulsa, Oklahoma

Momentum Builders:
228 Sure Fire Ways To Get on a Roll. . .and Stay There
ISBN 1-56292-082-0
Copyright © 1995 by John Mason
P.O. Box 54996
Tulsa, Oklahoma 74155

Published by Honor Books, Inc.
P.O. Box 55388
Tulsa, Oklahoma 74155

Introduction

Momentum — what a great word for a powerful life. I believe without a doubt that God's will for you is momentum. He wants you to let go of whatever makes you stop — to grow, to increase, to be more than what you are today.

These are the characteristics of momentum: 1) it is single-minded; 2) it is unwavering in the pursuit of a goal; 3) it has passion which knows no limits; 4) it demands a concentrated intensity and a definite sense of destiny; and, most of all, 5) it has a boundless vision and commitment to excellence.

As a result of reading and applying the nuggets in this book, I believe you will capture and increase momentum in your life. The Bible says you can be "confident of this very thing, that he which hath begun a good work in you will perform it until the day of Jesus Christ" (Phil. 1:6).

Be confident and receive God's momentum for your life.

John Mason

Don't waste time
waiting for inspiration.
Begin, and inspiration
will find you.

. . . . .

2

Be on a mission.

3

Never be afraid to do what
God tells you to do.

Many people fail in life because
they believe in the adage: "If you
don't succeed, try something else."

Don B. Owens, Jr.

. . . . .

Get out of the middle
of the road.

Be a creator of circumstances
not a victim of circumstances.

More men fail through lack
of purpose than lack of talent.

Billy Sunday

. . . . .

8

Think like a man of action
and act like a man of faith.

9

Know that your right action was
long ago approved by God.

It is better to fail in originality
than to succeed in imitation.

Herman Melville

. . . . .

Don't be denied,
you will find a way.

Don't let weeds grow
under your dreams.

If God is your partner...
make your plans BIG.

. . . . .

14

You can never trust
God too much.

15

Let prayer be the key
of your day and
the lock of your night.

Momentum Breaker
Indecision

Momentum Maker
Action

. . . . .

16

Know that nothing will ever be obtained
if all possible objections must first be overcome.

17

Attract others who are able to
help you achieve your goals.

Ideas are like rabbits. You get a couple
and learn how to handle them,
and pretty soon you have a dozen.

Anonymous

. . . . .

19

See success where others
see only failure.

20

See that the best opportunities
are hidden near you.

21

If you're not sure where you are going,
you'll probably end up someplace else.

Robert F. Mager

. . . . .

22

Never mistake knowledge for wisdom.

23

When God tells you to do
something, don't talk back!

Never let the fear of striking out
get in your way.

(Babe Ruth, strike out king, home run king).

. . . . .

25

Use the advice you give to others.

26

Specialize in the impossible.

Since it doesn't cost a dime to dream,
you'll never short-change yourself
when you stretch your imagination.

Robert Schuller

. . . . .

28

Act from your passions.

29

Cast all your cares upon God
because He cares for you.

Remember, the moment you say, "I give up," someone else is seeing the same situation and saying, "My, what a great opportunity."

. . . . .

31

Find happiness by
helping others find it first.

32

Assign yourself the task
of making someone happy.

The best way to accelerate your success is to double your failure rate. The law of failure is one of the most powerful of all success laws.

. . . . .

34

Know that enthusiasm
makes everything different.

35

Have no limits.

When you discover your mission, you will feel
its demand. It will fill you with enthusiasm
and a burning desire to get to work on it.

W. Clement Stone

. . . . .

37

Never chase a lie.

38

Never laugh at
anyone's dreams.

39

Don't let anybody steal your dream.

Dexter Yager

. . . . .

40

Use the past as a springboard,
not a hammock.

41

Become more and more
willing to risk failure.

Momentum Breaker
Fear

Momentum Maker
Faith

. . . . .

42

Remember, excuses
always replace progress.

43

The word "can't" really
means you won't try.

People judge you by your actions,
not your intentions. You may have a heart
of gold, but so does a hard boiled egg.

Good Reading

. . . . .

45

All roads to success
are uphill.

46

Your determination
creates time and opportunity.

47

You can't build a reputation
on what you're going to do.

Henry Ford

. . . . . .

48

Know that yesterday
ended last night.

49

Talk back to
your internal critic.

50

Show me someone who has done something worthwhile, and I'll show you someone who has overcome adversity.

Lou Holtz

. . . . .

51

Every now and then
bite off more than you can chew.

52

Expect resistance, criticism
and doubt, but don't stop.

53

It's not the mountains we conquer,
but ourselves.

Sir Edmond Hillary

. . . . .

Pursue character before prosperity.

Be loyal to all those who depend on you.

56

Every problem has in it the seeds of
its own solution. If you don't have
any problems, you don't get any seeds.

Norman Vincent Peale

. . . . .

57

If you are made of the right stuff,
a hard fall results in a sky-high bounce.

58

Never, never, never quit.

Show me a thoroughly satisfied man
and I will show you a failure.

.

Thomas Edison

. . . . .

60

Know that setbacks
pave the way for comebacks.

61

Be ready, now!

Momentum Breaker
The Past

Momentum Maker
Dreams

. . . . .

62

Prefer the foolishness of enthusiasm
to the indifference of logic.

63

Be sincerely interested
in helping others.

64

Do the right thing at the right time.
A Chinese proverb says, "Never leave
your field in spring or your house in winter."

. . . . .

65

Keep your friendships
in constant repair.

66

Do small things
in a great way.

A belief is not just an idea a person possesses;
it is an idea that possesses a person.

. . . . .

68

Be quick to take
advantage of an advantage.

69

Remember, procrastination is
the devil's number one strategy.

The characteristics of momentum:
1) it is single-minded;
2) it is unwavering in the pursuit of a goal;
3) it has passion which knows no limits;
4) it demands a concentrated intensity and
a definite sense of destiny; and, most of all,
5) it has a boundless vision and
commitment to excellence.

. . . . .

71

Don't anticipate trouble.

72

Don't confuse "bad luck"
with destiny.

The common conception is that motivation
leads to action, but the reverse is true —
action precedes motivation.

Robert McKain

. . . . .

74

Determine what you want.

75

Make a decision before
you have to make one.

You are the same today that you are
going to be in five years from now except
for two things: the people with whom
you associate and the books you read.

Charlie "Tremendous" Jones

. . . . .

Never decide to do nothing
just because you can only
do a little.

Do what you can.

Momentum Breaker
Tradition

Momentum Maker
Creativity

. . . . .

79

Learn the rules.
Then break some.

80

Avoid following the crowd.

Why worry about things you can't control?
Get busy controlling the things
that depend upon you.

In a Nutshell

. . . . .

82

Make God your hope,
not your excuse.

83

Nothing can make you feel
so strong as a call to God for help.

Opportunities multiply as they are seized;
they die when neglected.

Anonymous

. . . . .

85

Better is possible,
good is not enough.

86

Know "why",
not just "how."

The guy who gets ahead is the guy who does more than is necessary — and keeps doing it. No matter how rough the path, you cannot fulfill your destiny on what you intend to do.

. . . . . .

88

Surround yourself with
people smarter than you.

89

Don't stop the parade
to pick up a penny.

Give so much time to the improvement
of yourself that you have no time
to criticize others.

Optimist Creed

. . . . .

91

He who dares nothing
should expect nothing.

92

Do something that you
don't have to do.

93

One who is contented with what he has done
will never be famous for what he will do.

Christian Bovee

. . . . .

94

Don't wait for the perfect moment.

95

Don't beat yourself.
Don't build a case
against yourself.

96

Success, real success, in any endeavor
demands more from an individual than
most people are willing to offer — not
more than they are capable of offering.

James Roche

. . . . .

97

Paths with no obstacles
don't lead anywhere.

98

Know that quality
is never an accident.

99

The critic is convinced that the chief
purpose of sunshine is to cast shadows.

. . . . .

100

Keep your goals
out of reach,
but not out of sight.

101

Concentrate all your energies
on a limited set of targets.

102

You'll never succeed beyond your
wildest dreams unless you
have some wild dreams.

. . . . .

103

Dare to think
unthinkable thoughts.

104

Take your mind off
the things that seem
to be against you.

Momentum Breaker
Unforgiveness

Momentum Maker
Compassion

. . . . .

105

Don't delegate your thinking,
dreaming or believing.

106

If at first you don't succeed,
try something harder.

107

When you leave God out, you'll find yourself without any invisible means of support. Great things are achieved by those who dare to believe that God inside them is superior to circumstances.

. . . . .

108

You are destined
to be different.

109

Learn how to
fail intelligently.

110

A small man stands on others.
A great man stands on God.

. . . . .

111

Gain the advantage
by doing things before
they need to be done.

112

Desire more than you can accomplish.

Those who think it is permissible to tell
"white lies" soon grow colorblind.

Awson O'Malley

. . . . .

114

Welcome change
as a friend.

115

Change everything
except your loves.

116

If we live truly, we shall truly live.

Ralph Waldo Emerson

. . . . .

117

Believe in miracles.

118

Love will find a way.
Everything else will find an excuse.

As the sun makes ice melt,
kindness causes misunderstanding,
mistrust and hostility to evaporate.

. . . . .

120

Be a good finder.

121

Have a low tolerance
for idleness.

122

Friends in your life are like pillars
on your porch: Sometimes they hold you up;
sometimes they lean on you; sometimes
it's just enough to know they're standing by.

Anonymous

. . . . .

123

Create an atmosphere
of forgiveness.

124

Learn from the mistakes
of others.

Momentum Breaker
Double-mindedness

Momentum Maker
Focus

. . . . .

125

Never reject forgiveness.

126

Make your word your bond.

127

He who fiddles around seldom
gets to lead the orchestra.

. . . . .

128

Get ahead during the time
that others waste.

129

Never claim a
victory prematurely.

130

God never built a Christian strong enough
to carry today's duties and tomorrow's
anxieties piled on top of them.

Theodore Ledyard Cuyler

. . . . .

131

Be yourself, and the
person you hope to be.

132

Expect to win.

Practical prayer is harder on the soles of your shoes than on the knees of your trousers.

Osten O'Malley

. . . . .

134

Say "next time,"
not "if only."

135

Don't belittle,
be BIG!

Those who can see God's hand in everything
can leave everything in God's hands.

. . . . .

137

When you stop to think,
don't forget to start again.

138

If possible, make
the decision now.

139

A day hemmed in prayer
is less likely to unravel.

Anonymous

. . . . .

140

Have your own style.

141

Find a reason
why you "can."

142

The world has rarely seen what God
can do with, for and through a man
who is completely yielded to Him.

. . . . .

143

Follow your own star.

144

Don't be afraid to
ask dumb questions.

145

God created the world out of nothing,
and as long as we are nothing,
He can make something out of us.

Martin Luther

. . . . .

146

Stay incurably curious.

147

Take massive action on
creative and useful ideas.

148

Prayer may not change all things for you,
but it sure changes you for all things.
Prayer is the stop that keeps you going.

. . . . .

149

Leave the beaten path occasionally
and drive in the woods.

150

It's passion that persuades.

Momentum Breaker
Jealousy

Momentum Maker
Wisdom

. . . . .

151

Don't put worst things first.

152

Let God's Word shine on your worries.

153

You're not free until you've been made captive
by God's supreme plan for your life.

. . . . .

154

Don't spend your life answering
a question nobody's asking.

155

Do what people say you can't do.

156

Don't let regrets replace your dreams.

. . . . .

157

Be an expert at "why,"
not "why not".

158

Do more than is
required of you.

159

Keep your eye on the road, and use your
rear-view mirror only to avoid trouble.

Daniel Meacham

. . . . .

160

Give what you should.

161

Be aggressively thankful.

162

Don't make the mistake of letting
yesterday use up too much of today.

. . . . .

163

Know what to overlook.

164

Learn to say "no" to the good,
so you can say "yes" to the great.

165

Faith is not a pill you take but a muscle
you use. Faith is when your hands
and feet keep on working when your
head and others say it can't be done.

. . . . .

166

Be uncommon,
use common sense.

167

If at first you do succeed,
try something harder.

Momentum Breaker
Conformity

Momentum Maker
Change

. . . . .

168

Be unpopular when necessary.

169

The quickest way for you to
get a lot of things accomplished
is to do just one thing at a time.

170

A man is not old until regrets
take the place of dreams.

John Barrymore

. . . . .

171

Never be without
an important goal.

172

Regrets look back.
Worry looks around.
Faith looks up.

If you refuse to accept anything
but the best, you very often get it.

W. Somerset Maugham

. . . . .

174

One hour today is
worth two tomorrow.

175

Take time to pray when
you don't have time for it.

176

Prayer is asking for rain;
faith is carrying the umbrella.

. . . . .

177

Commit yourself to a dream.

178

Concentrate only on
things in your control.

Faith is like a flashlight: no matter how dark it gets, it will help you find your way. Every tomorrow has two handles; we can take hold by the handle of anxiety or by the handle of faith.

Southern Baptist Brotherhood Journal

. . . . .

Simply wait on God.

Stop and daydream
once in a while.

182

With God's strength behind you, His love with
you and His arms underneath you, you are
more than sufficient for the days ahead of you.

. . . . .

183

Nothing is easy to the unwilling.

184

It takes the hammer of persistence
to drive the nail of success.

Three strategies for success:
1) a big waste basket — you must know
what to eliminate;
2) know what to preserve;
3) know when to say no, for developing the
power to say no gives us the capacity to say yes.

A.P. Goethe

. . . . .

186

Do unto others as though
you were the others.

187

Develop greatness in others.

Momentum Breaker
Dishonesty

Momentum Maker
Character

. . . . .

188

Cause something to happen.

189

When you stumble today,
pick yourself up tomorrow.

190

Give the man you'd like to be
a look at the man you are.

Edgar Guest

. . . . .

191

Live your life and
forget your age.

192

Know that the starting point
for all achievement is desire.

Success really is simply a matter of doing
what you do best and not worrying about
what the other person is going to do.
You carry success or failure within yourself.
It does not depend on outside conditions.

. . . . .

194

If you find yourself in a hole,
stop digging!

195

Always have the courage to
face the truth.

196

Truth is always strong, no matter
how weak it looks, and falsehood is always
weak no matter how strong it looks.

Marcus Antioninus

. . . . .

197

Do the one thing you
really ought to do.

198

Keep your heart right even
when it's sorely wounded.

199

The way each day will look to you
starts with who you're looking to.

. . . . .

200

Eliminate from your life those
who belittle your unique ambitions.

201

Believe that now is the best time
to be alive and productive.

You'll find that life is an uphill battle
for the person who's not on the level.

Joan Welsh

. . . . .

203

When your strategy is hit or miss,
you'll usually miss.

204

There are people who will always come up
with reasons why you can't do what
you dream to do. Ignore them.

Momentum Breaker
Ingratitude

Momentum Maker
Giving

. . . . .

205

Stop being ashamed of what you believe.

206

Never let up when you are ahead.

It makes all the difference in the world
whether we put truth in the first place
or in the second place.

John Morley

. . . . .

208

Find unsuccessful people
you know and do the opposite.

209

Your first words every morning
should be, "Here I am, send me."

210

Excellence measures a man by the height
of his ideals, the breadth of his compassion,
the depth of his convictions and the length
of his persistence. People will always
determine your character by observing
what you stand for, fall for and lie for.

. . . . .

211

Don't deliberately plan to be less
than you are capable of being.

212

Allow right actions and divine order
to control and dominate your life.

213

We don't need more strength or more
ability or greater opportunity.
What we need to use is what we have.

Basil Walsh

. . . . .

214

Make at least one person happy
each day of your life.

215

Know that you can always do the
very best you can where you are
with what you have.

216

The grandest things are, in some ways,
the easiest to do because there is
so little competition.

. . . . .

217

Tackle a problem that is bigger than you.

218

When you think you're in the groove,
you're most often in a rut.

About the Author

John Mason is the founder and president of Insight International, an organization dedicated to encouraging people to use all their gifts and talents while fulfilling God's plan for their lives.

He is in much demand throughout the United States and abroad as a speaker and minister. He is the author of several best-selling books, as well as many tape and video series.

John, his wife Linda, and their four children — Michelle, Greg, Mike, and Dave — currently reside in Orlando, Florida.

John welcomes the opportunity to minister at your church, conference, retreat, or in men's, women's, and youth groups.

Send all prayer requests and inquiries to:

Insight International
P.O. Box 54996
Tulsa, Oklahoma 74155

Dear Reader:

If you would like to share with us a couple of your favorite quotes or ideas on the subject of *building momentum in every area of your life*, we would love to hear from you. Our address is:

Honor Books
P.O. Box 55388
Tulsa, Oklahoma 74155

Other titles by John Mason

An Enemy Called Average
You're Born an Original — Don't Die a Copy
Let Go of Whatever Makes You Stop
Don't Wait for Your Ship To Come In...Swim Out to Meet It!
Words of Promise

are available at your local bookstores.

P.O. Box 55388
Tulsa, Oklahoma 74155